3 Wishes
Text Guide Edition
Personalised Colouring Book
Vision Board Tool
(Non Visual Edition)

A.O.K. McKenzie

ISBN: 1544617798
ISBN-13: 978-154461779

DEDICATION

I dedicate this book to anybody who has ever lost their way.
By starting with a clear vision and end in mind, I hope this book helps
you be found.

CONTENTS

ACKNOWLEDGMENTS

My thanks always to Infinite Intelligence.

With the deepest gratitude I thank everyone who touched my life, you helped illuminate me to the point of conceiving this work.

Special thanks to my father, my ideal teacher on how to dream.

INTRODUCTION

Your wish is my command! Welcome to a new image of you! 3 Wishes is a personalised visual tool that will help give you a clear image of what wishes, dreams or goals you want in life. The complete 3 Wishes personalised colouring book vision board tool is made up of a text guide section and an images section. We created these personalised art wish images to bring you a powerful visualization tool. Whichever 3 Wishes book edition you have will help shine a light on how to bring your wishes to life using the power of personalised images.

3 Wishes Aims

This personalised book tool aims to arouse within you a more passionate dedication to the wish manifestation process. A more personal connection will enable you to get to your goals much quicker than if you were using non-personalised methods. As you are highly engaged in these personalised images your imagination and belief will be activated on higher levels which will bring better wish manifestation results. High engagement is achieved by passionately colouring in and immersing yourself in these wish images.

Another of the 3 Wishes aims is to help you bring your wishes to life by strongly impressing upon you a new self-image and subconscious belief. We also aim to evoke within you a strong sense of self-belief and self-love that will help bring your energy into alignment with your desires.

Further aims of this book are to serve as a refocusing energy healing guide that touches upon mindfulness themes. Anytime your energy feels low or off-track come back to this book and reread a few encouraging pages from the text guide section. When you feel like being active use the images activity section and add in some more colour and dimension to your wish images. Or have a mental workout by spending some time meditating on and visualising your wish images.

So can you think up your wish, colour in your wish, really feel your wish, see your wish and then through your efforts bring your wish into existence? Yes you can! This is dream working in action! Good Luck and here's to the Dreamers!

THE ALCHEMIST'S ELEMENTS

An alchemist is someone who transforms or creates using a seemingly magical process. Alchemy usually involves transforming something ordinary into the extraordinary, for example changing lead into gold or water into wine. The wish manifestation process is alchemy in action because through it we take our intangible desires and transform them into our dream lives. This makes you an alchemist in training! Every good alchemist needs to know what elements to use to achieve a successful transformation and when to use them. The following sections discuss the main elements involved in the wish manifestation process.

Starting With the End in Mind

Starting with the end in mind means you are beginning a task with a clear vision of your desired goal and using this vision to motivate you. In providing you with an vision of your end goal we have brought you one step closer to your dreams by granting your wishes on paper. These wish images will help you **see** anything is possible for you! In this personalised art book as you see yourself in the wish images and colour them in you are starting to bring your vision to life. By focusing your attention on your wish images you breathe your life into them and you colour in, what could very well be, your whole new world into existence.

Say your wish is to graduate from University and the wish image we have created is of you smiling wearing your cap and gown. As you sit down to colour in this image you begin by selecting your colour pencils, questions may pop into your head like "What colour is my dress going to be on graduation day? Hmm, I think I'll wear my favourite red dress. Ok I'll use the red pencil." What happened here when you mixed real life with dream life? For a second a part of your mind really thought "I'm graduating today, what will I wear?" A train of like thoughts latch on to that thought and start to grow, then all of a sudden it's like you are already graduating in your mind! On some level you are have already reached your end goal. The more you consistently engage with anything the more a part of your being accepts on some level that thing is real. A part of your mind imprints your wish image and a stream of mental energy starts to build it up into reality.

Listen To Your Heart

How do you know what you want your wish image to be? You find out by asking and listening to your intelligent heart! The heart element is essential in the wish manifestation process because it can provide wise counsel. By using this 3 Wishes book tool you ask yourself "What wishes do I want? What are my heart desires?" You have started to really think, listen and connect with your precious heart.

Sometimes we may not even want to try to dream because we are protecting ourselves from disappointments, we are scared of heartbreak. Too often we don't even let ourselves dream because our dreams just seem so far away from our current circumstances. When we do occasionally break free and allow ourselves to think about our dreams negative thoughts may get in the way saying "What's the use, where would I even start from anyway?" You start by just listening to your heart, not the fear.

Fear has a lot to answer for in life, fear has sent a lot of exquisite wishes to the graveyard of broken dreams prematurely. The saddest thing about that is most of our fears are unfounded, in most cases fear is just our minds running away with themselves. That is why it is important to remember we are not our thoughts and we can shift fearful thoughts.

Just imagine for just one minute that there is nothing to be afraid of really, that there are no monsters and that your wise heart could not be broken. How would you go about living your life then? Would you then finally listen to your brilliant heart and hear what it has to say? As you ponder this deeply breathing in that fearless air, imagine what of your wishes fulfilled life would look like in an image.

Crystal Clear Image

3 Wishes will provide clarity on what you really want in life, this clarity will make it easier to bring your desires into reality. Clarity of focus also makes it easier to live our lives with purpose, as opposed to just letting life's distractions run the show.

In this age of information overload life can get foggy with so many distractions..hang on a sec, let me check my phone..(sic) So many things relentlessly compete daily for your attention. Academic research shows we are distracted on average every 3 minutes! It can then take us up to 11 minutes to really re-gain and re-focus our attention. This lost time starts to really add up and could ultimately destroy our chances of true happiness in this lifetime. If we do not learn to keep distractions in check, then despite our best intentions there may be literally no time left in our days, months and years for our dreams.

As we begin to see the real subtle danger here it becomes apparent that without a clear vision people really can perish in distractions. If we are not focused on our own goals these distractions can easily overwhelm us and make us sidetracked.

So how can we take back control and focus on our goals better? We need something to focus our attention on in order to take our minds off distractions. By starting to hold on tightly on to a crystal clear image of what you wish for yourself every single day you are steadily changing your focus and thus priorities. You give yourself a new vision so you are no longer drowning in distractions.

This crystal clear image or vision is your personalised wish image in this book. This is your new vision for yourself. What we focus on expands, so as you cling tightly to your wish image you may find there is more space in your life for your goals and less space for distractions. A crystal clear vision for yourself gives you the defence that you need to help fight off distractions. Focusing on your personal vision can inspire you on how to best manage your time and energy.

A consistent, determined, persistent focus on our goals will soon result in our desires, energies and manifestations all coming into alignment with each other. When there is alignment we can't help but take action, consciously or unconsciously, towards our dreams. This is how dreams can start to come true!

Keeping Your Inner Child Alive

Alchemists need all the magic and fairy dust they can get, so begin to allow yourself to dream like you once did as a child. If you are a child reading this then don't lose that trusting belief, keep it up! To bring our dreams to life as adults we must break free from cynicism. We must literally tear down neural pathways of cynicism that life has built up in our heads over time. This process is akin to pressing the reset button and putting ourselves through a mental and emotional detox. Now that would be a fantastic way to kick-start the new year along with our physical health kicks!

We must reclaim our innocence through wisdom and this time intuitively know that your heart cannot be broken. Because life's pain and hurts have happened perhaps you have long since buried your wishes and dreams. Perhaps you thought that they were child's play, but underneath it all your desires are still there and they will keep on coming. Your heart desires are in you for a reason, trust that! Do not listen to anyone, including yourself, telling you to forget about your dreams because of your past mistakes!

Dream Power

Dream power is an essential element in the wish manifestation process because you need to believe in your dreams first before they even have a chance of coming true.

As children we had unblemished dream power in our hearts, an innocence and complete faith that gave us undiluted energy. As we got older, unfortunately, others may not have responded to our dreams in a supportive fashion. In fact some people may have even trampled all over our dreams telling us to "Stop dreaming!" and "Get your head out of the clouds!" These negative reactions can be hurtful, confusing and distracting so let's try to understand what could be behind them.

There are many reasons why dreams produce such strong reactions in people. Perhaps it is because dream power is an extra special fuel that can project you forward past others in life, so some people may feel threatened. Some people may get scared you will leave them behind and may even get jealous. Or it could be because when you really believe in your dreams you will just know deep down that you are going somewhere in life! Because of this deep knowing you find that you walk with a little more dignity, you have direction in life and you don't waste your time with distractions. When you live your life with purpose like this, others may feel sad because they know deep down that they don't feel that same loving way about themselves.

To bring you down to their level, some people may remind you of all your past missteps. They may say to you, "Don't you remember where you are from? You've just made too many mistakes in the past!" These misguided people may advise you, "You'll never make it so just forget about your dreams!" Doesn't it make you wonder what all the fuss is about? If your dreams are really so worthless, and meant to be just thrown away, then why such strong emotional reactions from people?

Now sometimes this can all come from a place of protection and them genuinely not wanting you to get disappointed. But others do not know your true power only you do! What didn't work out for them might actually work out for you. What these people do not seem to realise is that regardless of their own disappointments in life, they still have some dreams and desires buried inside them too. Their own dreams could happen for them, but only if they would stop throwing dirt on themselves and others! If only these naysayers would put that same energy that they use to belittle others into positivity instead and love themselves they could change their subconscious beliefs.

Perhaps these folks have caused you pain, do not hate them, they often carry deep emotional wounds and unconsciously operate from limited mindsets. Hate consumes too much energy and remember people do not determine your destiny anyway. Send these confused people light, hopefully one day they will learn to do better and truly love themselves. Then turn your attention back onto yourself and focus on you building your passion back up, getting your own energy back on track.

In life, I have found, if you do not hold on tightly to a belief that your dreams can come true it becomes very easy to start to degrade yourself. If you don't believe you can have what you truly want thoughts may pop into your head like "Well what's the point in really trying at life anyway? I just can't have what I really want." Your natural energy flow becomes misaligned and your energy stream starts to split up. With no real life passion or purpose it becomes easy to start to just let anything and everything happen to you. This is why our belief in our dreams is incredibly important and is worth fighting for. The belief in our dreams sets the tone for our quality of life, essentially it is the difference between leading a passionless or a passion full life. It is for this reason that dream power is very important, it is something we must protect and nurture.

So far we have seen the benefits of starting with the end in mind, listening to our heart, having a crystal clear wish image, keeping our inner child alive and protecting our dream power in the wish manifestation process. What force can we use to bind all these elements together? The powerful natural law of attraction!

Law of Attraction & Planning

To explain the law of attraction it is important to first state that this Universe operates in terms of interrelated energy, frequency and vibration.

"If you wish to understand the universe, think in terms of energy, frequency and vibration."

Nikola Tesla

As humans we are vibrational beings that operate, consciously or unconsciously, on different frequencies or energy fields. We can change what frequency or energy field we want to operate on by changing our thoughts and emotions. It has been scientifically proven that our thoughts and emotions give off measureable electromagnetic frequencies via our brainwaves. Different types of thoughts and emotions create different types of brainwaves that transmit electromagnetic alpha, theta or delta frequencies. People are always transmitting their frequencies this is partly why we can pick up on someone's vibe, for example, when they step into the room. As vibrational beings the particular electromagnetic frequency we emit will determine what will be magnetised back to us in the real world because of the incredibly methodical law of attraction.

The law of attraction is a powerful natural law or force governing this planet. Essentially the law of attraction states that <u>like attracts like,</u> <u>thoughts become things</u> and <u>you will get what you focus on</u>. The law of attraction says that in life we will get what we think the about the most and we will also become what we think about most. The law of attraction also says that if you focus on anything with a lot of passion then you get more of that thing showing up more quickly in your life. Essentially we are mobile magnets attracting our life experiences into our reality through the electromagnetic frequencies our thoughts and feelings generate. According to these definitions how can we then use this law or force to make our wishes come true?

To manifest using the law of attraction you have to be what you wish for in order to attract it into your life. Also you have to think strong thoughts that your wish has already being granted in order to make it show up as a real thing in your life. Now as you can imagine applying the law of attraction can be a bit of a tricky thing to do, because your wish is not currently manifested in your life but yet you have to strongly believe that it is real in order to attract it in. You are essentially bending reality with your mind. All these practices become easier to do when you have a clear image of yourself already living your dream that you can focus upon, that is the wish image you have in this book.

Let's look at the law of attraction in a wish manifestation example, say someone has been having an experience of financial lack. So how could they use their 3 Wishes wish image and the law of attraction to manifest their wish of becoming financially abundant? That person must practice being abundant by making themselves feel the emotion of abundance, so they can emit electromagnetic frequencies of abundance, in order to then attract abundance into their life. They have to give to receive. They have to work themselves up to the emotional state of feeling abundant first to attract financial abundance into their life. They can do this by really imagining and thinking of themselves as rich so they can begin to feel rich and emit abundance frequencies. They must really get into the feeling rich role by imagining themselves living a rich lifestyle with cars, houses and other symbols of wealth.

Seeing themselves in a new abundant way will also shift their self-image from that of solely defining themselves as always being in lack, to a new self-image of being abundant. This soon becomes a virtuous circle of attraction because seeing themselves in this new abundant way helps them think more calmly, objectively and clearly. Their liberated way of thinking will attract in an abundance of new ideas as their imagination is no longer shut down because of their heavy focus on lack. You must first free your mind before you can see results in the real world.

No matter what their current financial situation is that person's wholehearted focus and attention must never be on lack. Their main focus must always be on what it is they actually want, which is abundance. Their deep focus must not be on observing and defining themselves by their current financial circumstances because if it is, according to the law of attraction, they will doom themselves to attracting only more of the same.

In the law of attraction different types of emotions emit different strengths of vibrations that either help or hinder our wish manifestation. Positive emotions like happy, grateful and confident give off strong vibrations that strongly magnetize things to us. Fear and doubt are negative emotions which are counterproductive to our actual desires. Likewise positive thoughts give off stronger frequencies than negative thoughts. If you have a negative thought, don't add worry to that thought because this emotion of worry carries a negative charge that actually makes your negative thought worse. To deal with negative thoughts essentially override them by intentionally switching your focus to positive thoughts. Do this as soon as you notice a negative thought because those negative thoughts can soon become negative emotions. Negativity repels, it will take you further away from what it is you actually want.

As you change the way you think and feel you will find yourself full of new ideas, and so you can start to make an action plan on how to bring your dreams to life. Some dreams will need a big plan and sometimes a small plan will do. Sometimes not much of a plan is required and because of your strong feelings the law of attraction just naturally brings your wish to you. Just be open to the Universe.

What You Must Know For Sure

Your dreams are where your belief, faith, attention, focus and energy should actually be going. Your focus, belief and faith should not be invested in distractions and fear. Allow your wishes and dreams to come out in full colour in these pages, breathe your wonderful unique life energy into these wish images. Your dreams are your extra special fuel in this life and you must fight for them! You never know these dreams could be great joys tailor-made just for you, and YOU my dear are VERY, VERY IMPORTANT!

YOU'VE ALWAYS HAD THE POWER

Believe it or not each of us is walking around with a genie on the inside zapping away! You don't need to go and look for a symbolic lamp to rub or get yourself some magic slippers, we all have that power already inside us. To be happy and harness this power our genies just need a bit of guidance. This book will give your genie the direction they need, 3 Wishes will provide your genie somewhere solid to start from on your wish manifestation journey.

It is important to know what you are working with before beginning any endeavour. An alchemist magically transforms something ordinary into the extra-ordinary, how do they really know that they can do this and how can you know this for yourself? It all starts with you understanding your own innate power!

Know Thyself

This book is titled 3 Wishes in a nod to a much loved Arabian Nights story. But the reality is, as you may have already guessed, in life we get a lot more than three wishes. Thank Goodness! Even when we think we've blown it and we have just made too many mistakes we can always get more wishes, that is of course if we believe we can.

In the popular film of the Aladdin tale the moral of the story is that the real power and magic is inside each of us, because our personal self-worth and self-love triumphs external riches. Although he had power inside himself all along Aladdin was not consciously aware of it, nor did he believe in himself. He did not really know himself because he was not aware of his own inherent power. Through a series of adventures Aladdin had to learn that he had something inside so strong and he also had to learn how to use his power with confidence.

This power and magic inside us is made up of many forces that can all come together to do our biddings. To understand the nature of the team of forces that aid wish manifestation in particular, let's start off by discussing the star player on the team, imagination!

Imagination

Imagination is our mental creative faculty that uses images to form new ideas that are not yet apparent to the senses. Imagination is the ability your mind has to form an idea of something that is not yet real in the physical. Imagination is an invisible creative force that we can access at anytime 24/7, 365 days of the year! In our absolute uniqueness we are each designed to overcome predicaments we face in life if we can utilise our imagination.

Strong imagination has been used time and time again to survive terrible ordeals. Survivors of concentration camps used imagination to endure horrific physical ordeals. Their strong imagination helped them get through and eventually survive the camp. These people attributed their survival to the strong imagining of themselves becoming free again. Despite the awful conditions that surrounded them, they mentally empowered themselves by powerfully dreaming their wish for freedom outside of the camp. Some people even coped by imagining they were actors undercover play acting in that experience. Imagination can work many ways, the point is they did not mentally stagnate in the image of being a concentration camp prisoner forever. Their imagination was an invisible force that they could not physically see in the camp, but it still served them well enough to help them overcome very real terrible physical circumstances.

Imagination will serve you as much as you believe it will. Here it served these survivors so much that it helped them physically endure inhumane conditions and they eventually made it out the other side alive. This true life example means imagination can be used to accomplish even physical survival against all odds. Don't you wonder how imagination can serve you just in your everyday life? Just imagine if you begin to purposefully tap into this creative force, how much more could imagination boost and increase your life?

Imagination is abundantly free, a multifaceted tool that we universally share as humans, from children to pensioners. Your imagination can change everything in your world through the force of the law of attraction. Imagination can elevate you to great fame and fortune even securing you a firm place in history.

"Imagination is more important than knowledge"

Albert Einstein

Albert Einstein was a famous great scientist. What set him apart from other great scientists and what earned him an indisputable place in the history books were his methods, most notably his fantastic utilisation of his imagination. Einstein often used his imagination and daydreaming to solve his scientific problems. He often referred to himself as an artist because a part of imagination Einstein always utilized was creative thinking. Through a complex process he often solved his science problems not by the traditional way of writing things down but by the use of images in his head. He used his imagination to form mental images in order to work out solutions to scientific questions. Along the way he trusted in his intuition, that is a sense of knowing, to help guide him in the right direction. Only later on in the process would he then eventually write these solutions down into words or equations. During the process he often *felt* he was right (notice like attracting like here) in his workings even before his theory (that was his wish to solve the science problem) was proven correct by other scientists, at which point it was then externally confirmed he was right (his wish came true).

Just like Einstein you too must *think*, *feel* and *know* that what you have imagined (your wish) has already come true in order to attract it as a real thing into your life in the third dimension. This is a true life example of a famous scientist using images, imagination and the law of attraction to grant his wishes, this is genius creative thinking in action! This same process can be applied to any field of endeavour. In his scientific problem solution process Einstein felt strongly he was right and this often attracted the right solution to him. It was a virtuous circle of attraction.

It is my belief that because Einstein dedicated a lot of his time to intense imagining and day dreaming, this is how he was able to build up his imagination muscle. He built it up to the point that he could even begin to tap into the Universal Mind whilst still awake in his daydreams. The Universal Mind is the pure stream of knowing all that is. Because of his methods and practices Einstein was able to tap into this stream of supreme energy. Universal Mind was able to provide him with answers and insight that other great scientists did not have access to, because they did not use the same creative mental methods. There will be more on the Universal Mind later on.

It is very worth while pausing here and making a side note on intuition, as is mentioned in the Einstein example. Intuition is the ability to understand something instinctively, this understanding often comes without a need for conscious or logical reasoning. Intuition was essential in Einstein's creative process, his intuition guided his work and it required from him his openness and trust. Trusting in intuition can be likened to letting go and floating on water. It takes practice to sharpen our intuition but it is highly worth doing so because intuition can help you solve many mysteries, just like Sherlock Holmes. Often it is only after we ignore our intuition, and see the repercussions of this, that we eventually learn how to really listen.

Our imagination must be trained, why must it be trained? It must be trained because it is a force that can work for us or against us. Imagination can be trained in many ways. One way to train your imagination is to get it to only focus on the things you actually want, e.g. security or love, and not imagine the opposite. A lot of people counterproductively spend their time worrying and imagining things getting worse, so by law, that is exactly what they will then attract into their life. Another way imagination can be trained is to make it strong enough to be able to conjure up real feelings and emotions inside you. When trained up your imagination can become so strong that it can actually change your mood, thus changing your emitted frequency. Your imagination can be built up to become so strong that when you switch it on no matter what your physical surroundings are, it is as if you become no longer mentally present there. Because you are imagining great things for yourself mentally, this can have the effect of making you feel removed from a bad situation and can make you feel better which then goes on to attract better things to you.

Imagination is a truly powerful force that can manifest real life effects even if we intend them or not. Imagination without a purpose produces effects in the real physical world all the time. We've all had this experience of just thinking about a friend you haven't spoken to in a while, just idly imagining what they are getting up to. Then all of a sudden that same friend you were thinking about sends you a message or perhaps a couple of days later you hear from them! Don't you wonder what in life makes this work? How can this be, just a thought in your head of your friend draws that person to you?

It is almost as if through imagining you conjured up your friend's energy and then their matching energy came back to you like a boomerang. And because you did so in a spirit of least resistance, i.e. your feelings flowed with no complications, you saw real life results swiftly. So because in this world like energy attracts like energy, the law of attraction made that friend want to reach out to you in response to your mental daydream! Once you conjure up a particular frequency, that frequency's matching real life effect will show up some how in your life. This is how creation occurs.

What we focus on we get more of, so we must be careful what we put our focus on and what we give our attention to. When you look at your current circumstances(our real life effects) are you starting to realise that according to the results around you, that you must have in fact been unintentionally spending more of your time imagining what you don't want, rather than what you do actually want. You know consciously what you want, so what is really happening here? This will be addressed later.

Now naturally this may all be starting to sound rather concerning! We are starting to see how even just our thoughts and imagination can bring us effects that we don't actually want to see in the real world. But thankfully we do not need to monitor every single imagining because clearly not every single daydream will manifest. Typically what brings about big effects on our lives in the real world is prolonged powerfully felt thought. In other words, someone would need to think a lot of negative thoughts strongly and consistently enough to make them feel deeply negative to their core, it is this intensity of feeling that then brings about strong negative effects in their life.

With the average person having over 50,000 thoughts a day is there a simple way to stop our imagination from running wild? Yes, there is a powerful way we can gather and focus our thoughts and imaginings. It is through knowing how to use the power of images to our advantage.

The Power of Images

Images can help capture our imagination enabling us to keep it on track. Most of the time we don't think in words, as a visual species we think in images. There was a time in history when there was no common language shared amongst humans. We communicated and told stories using drawings or symbols like the Ancient Egyptian hieroglyphics. This strong image wiring is still very much present in us today that is why humans can process images 60,000 times more quickly than text. Knowing we have such strong reactions to images we can start to use our natural predisposition to our own personal advantage, like so many organisations do already.

Visual images are excellent communicators because they quickly affect us on a deep psychological and emotional level. Perhaps this is why in advertising visuals are often regarded as shortcuts, this is as opposed to text which operates more linearly. Language itself can be limiting how many times have you heard "I just don't have the words to describe exactly how I'm feeling!" Different types of images can make us feel a certain type of emotion very quickly. Our instant emotional reaction to images means that they have more of an energetic impact on us. This makes images ideal for affecting, motivating, inspiring, influencing and invoking action. Even when learning, according to the Social Science Research Network, 65% of humans are visual learners. This is all partly because we can focus on, thus mentally imprint, an image more clearly than we can text. In short images significantly engage, activate and stimulate our mental and emotional faculties. Now how can we use this knowledge to our advantage?

An en masse example of how images still strongly affect us as humans is the news of today. Really think about what type of images are fed to us on our screens, newspapers, and magazines on a daily basis. The majority of daily news images and headlines are fear based and constantly focused on acts of terrorism, political or economic crisis, job uncertainty etc. In our media the overwhelming focus and attention is on promoting fear, insecurity, doubt and worry. Because we live in an information overload society, we now see even more of these negative images, they are always around us somewhere. Newton's Third Law tells us that for every action there is an equal reaction. So as we are now seeing a lot more of these negative images globally (the action) what could be a reaction equal to this? Is there anything else also happening globally that we are seeing a lot more of? Is there some rising global phenomenon that ties in with what we already know negative images can do to humans? You guessed it, stress! Stress is also a rising epidemic sweeping the globe, it is always around us somewhere and it is often the Number 1 root cause of health problems. The increase in our exposure to negative fear based images from the daily news, does significantly correlate with a wide spread increase of stress amongst humans. If humans are hardwired to be highly impressionable to images and then negative images are always in our face, then that has to bring about an equal reaction in our being somewhere.

Think about it, have you often watched the news just before going to sleep and then found that you just couldn't easily drift off or maybe your sleep was unsettled that night? But if you watched something positive or calming just before bed you would sleep fine. Just think about those two different types of images you are exposing yourself to. One type is negative and the other is positive, and think about what each type could be actually doing to your whole being.

"To play successfully the game of life, we must train the imaging faculty. A person with an imaging faculty trained to image only good, brings into his life every righteous desire of his heart – health, wealth, love, friends perfect self-expression, his highest ideals."

Florence Scovel Shinn

It is vital we understand what things might be present in our lives that are actually working against us and remove them in order to avoid frustration and disillusionment.

Now we are starting to get a real sense of the power that images have to influence us as human beings. This is good because in order to strengthen our wish manifestation efforts we must know ourselves and understand how to unlock our inherent power. We have discussed how imagination works and why we are naturally highly responsive to images, there is another way to pump up the effect images have on us even further! This is by use of personalised images.

The Extra Power of Personalised Images

By using personalised images we can invoke an even stronger energetic charge in ourselves, this allows us to summon up more of our inherent power.

Traditional vision boards are a great tool to look at for goal motivation. A personalised image gives us a personal vision that is even more powerful because we can actually see ourselves right there in our dream scenario or setting. Our personalised wish image enables us to put ourselves, more easily, in the emotional state of believing we already have our wish. Essentially as we see ourselves in the personalised wish image we buy into and emotionally invest more in our dream. We look at our wish image and we think, "Hey, that's me, this could be real. I could really go on that trip!" The intimacy of this emotional connection excites us more because we can see ourselves there. Personalisation leaves more of an impact on our emotions. The personalised wish images in this book help us get more into a strong state of belief that we have already achieved our goal. Our strong state of belief becomes a strong emotional charge which emits electromagnetic frequencies that go on to attract like results into our life. Personalised images inspire strong emotions in us, strong sustained emotions are the necessary catalyst that we need to affect real change. In order to conjure up powerful energy we need images that inspire ideas, arouse strong beliefs and evoke feelings.

When we are actively creative in personalised images, by colouring them in for example, we become even more engaged and influenced by them. As we colour in images we engage more with them because through this activity we are activating both sides of our brain. We create and we give the image even more of our attention and energy. Essentially an image becomes more soaked up in our subconscious mind when we are actively involved in it.

With most of the emphasis so far being on the mental realm, you can probably guess by now that wish manifestation starts in the mind. The change I refer to is not just a change of habits of thinking in our conscious mind, but also a change in our deeper subconscious mind. Highly personalised engagement is what we need to increase our chances of being able to change our deeply rooted subconscious beliefs. These beliefs must be tackled because it is these deeply held subconscious beliefs that we will see manifested in our lives on a large scale. Indeed we don't really get what we want in life, we get what we believe. So as an alchemist you need to be able to direct the power that lies in your subconscious.

The Subconscious

The subconscious is the part of your mind that lies dormant to your conscious or critical thought mind in your everyday interactions. However, your subconscious mind is incredibly more powerful than your conscious mind because it can process information at much more superior rate. Since birth our subconscious has been recording and processing every bit of information we have been exposed to. Unlike our conscious mind we are not always aware of what is going on in our unconscious mind, hence the name subconscious.

To get a clearer image of the scale of brain power that we are working with in our subconscious, picture an iceberg for a moment. Austrian neurologist and founder of psychoanalysis Sigmund Freud used the iceberg analogy to describe the subconscious. When we look at an iceberg what we can see poking out of the water is actually just the small tip of the iceberg (the tip represents the conscious mind) what is under the water is the much larger root of that iceberg (the root represents the vast subconscious mind).

Our subconscious houses all our stored information gathered over the course of our lifetime. This is why under hypnosis people can recall in great detail memories from years ago. It is because in this calm state their subconscious mind is being accessed and consulted not their error prone conscious mind. A lot of our deep-rooted, identity forming beliefs are stored in our subconscious mind. It is very important to pay attention to our subconscious mind because our subconscious beliefs drive most of our automatic pilot behaviour.

The subconscious thinks and speaks to us in feelings and images, which is another reason why we react so strongly to images. The subconscious regularly communicates with us in our dreams by use of images and symbolism. Images are the language of the subconscious and so we dream in images and feelings not paragraphs of text. When we dream often this is our subconscious communicating it's own thoughts to our conscious mind so we can remember these messages when we wake up.

The subconscious mind can reveal a wealth of knowledge and core beliefs inside us that we may not even be consciously aware of. For example, the subconscious could make you feel strongly drawn to a particular image but yet you do not fully comprehend why you feel so drawn to it. It is only after some time has passed and we have really dwelt upon this attraction does a revelation then finally dawn upon us. We are not always aware what our subconscious beliefs are, so sometimes our subconscious can try to let us know what they are by fixating our attention upon a particular image. The reason for this attraction might be that this particular image is an outward physical reflection of some internal emotional state. Or it could be a reflection of a deep-rooted subconscious belief within us that we are not even consciously aware of. Again we see here like attracting like, the law of attraction applies on so many levels!

Say you notice you are always drawn to images of lack and fear. Perhaps your subconscious is trying to let you know, that although you may not consciously know it, deep down on the inside you feel small and afraid. Our subconscious can also draw us to images that help us remember our hidden treasures and dreams. These could be images that re-affirm our core values and remind us of what things we should be prioritising and going for in life.

"As above, so below. As within, so without"

The Emerald Tablet

Your subconscious beliefs could be limiting you or empowering you, both will produce different results in life. To get an inkling of what your internal subconscious beliefs might be start to look around at the results that are manifested in your life. What is on the outside is also on the inside. What is really interesting is our subconscious beliefs may not always be what we consciously think they are. For example we may grow up consciously thinking "I'm going to be independent all my life" But then what is actually manifested in your life is you constantly finding yourself in dependent situations. So start to really look at your results in life to see what you are dealing with on a deeper level.

Our deep-rooted subconscious beliefs are built up over time and are often reinforced by the external world. Say for example, a person's subconscious belief and perception is "I can't trust anyone." Then that is the filter through which they will see and experience the world. Inevitably this person will get or attract more of the same distrusting experiences that they expect to see because that's right, like attracts like. Because their distrusting subconscious belief is so strong they will even misinterpret others kind actions towards them. Their subconscious belief will make this person even perceive the loving actions of the ones closest to them as being sneaky. You can see how things will never change in a person's life until they can actually see past a negative subconscious belief.

Because our subconscious talks to us in images we can also talk back or influence our subconscious through images. It stands to reason if you can use images to talk to your subconscious, you can also use images to adapt your subconscious beliefs A focused train of prolonged thought in your subconscious mind eventually leads to a subconscious belief being changed. It is a similar process to how we would change a negative belief in our conscious mind, that is by introducing a steady stream of positive thought. Changing your conscious and subconscious beliefs can help change the story you tell yourself about yourself.

In this wish manifestation process we have to be aware that we all have stories we tell ourselves about ourselves and self-talk. Self-talk is how we talk to ourselves, it's kind of like our own running commentary during our day or our internal conversation. You could have positive or negative self-talk each will produce different patterns of behaviour. During the day a person's story or self-talk could be "Everybody always picks on me." or "I'll never be good enough." If your story or self-talk is of this negative nature then you will most certainly limit yourself in life. You will become your own worst enemy that you cannot get away from. So it is in our own best interests to start today to make our self-talk and the story we tell ourselves more positive. In order to be happy and manifest what you want in life you do have to be your own cheerleader and cultivate love for yourself.

One of the 3 Wishes aims is to help change any negative self-image or negative concepts of self, these are also stored in the subconscious mind. If you currently have a negative self-image you are **not** stuck in it for life! Although your self-image is also deep-rooted it can change. Do not worry your self-image, self-talk and self-perception are not set in stone. These are all only the result of subconscious beliefs that have been formed from a train of consistent thoughts, conditioning or undirected mental programming. It will require deep work to change this programming but when you start to see yourself in a new light things will start to change, an energy shift does occur.

Did you know your mind does not only have access to the information you have been exposed to in this lifetime? Through your subconscious mind you also have access to the Universal Mind, the stream of knowing all that is. Wise people have always known this, that is why Einstein had his own methods to be able to tap into this resource. It is true you really do know more than you think you do.

As subconscious beliefs and concepts are deep-rooted, it can be challenging to see yourself differently and thereby start to change the story you tell yourself. However the truth will correct all errors that might have taken root in your mind. Remember science and medicine tells us all human beings are the same, no one is lesser or greater than the other. Every great tradition and theological doctrine tells us that we are all created in the image and the likeness of the

Creative Source. So with this knowledge you realise that in fact nothing is too good for you! Once you realise you are an extension of Source Energy you begin to see that this actually makes you a powerful creator. You begin to see that you are a spiritual being having a human experience. You are not here by accident so take control of your life now because you have always had the power!

To start to change a negative subconscious belief about yourself you can begin by feeding your subconscious reminders of the truth through images. These images could be the masterpieces in nature, beautiful art, images of hope, and positive images of yourself (like graduation pictures). Exposing yourself constantly to these positive images can begin to affect change from the outside in.

To change a negative subconscious belief about others you can start to focus on their positive aspects in order to start to see them positively. Essentially a conscious mental decision must be made to change what you focus on from that of negativity to positivity. Whatever you focus on with a lot of passion will grow. Your new positivity will grow until you remember subconsciously the truth about yourself and the truth about others, and the truth is that life is absolutely magnificent and so are you!

So start to correct errors and misjudgements in your subconscious mind, this will help you get closer to the glorious light of your dreams coming true. See yourself in these wish images living the life you want to live. Believe you can have it and believe you deserve it because in reality nothing is too good for you! Your wish image gives you a new image of yourself that you can focus your attention upon. The goal is that you no longer subconsciously see yourself in that same old way trapped in a limited concept of yourself. You have to have a new positive self-image to focus on in order to let go of a negative self-image. You have to see the light at the end of the tunnel to get yourself out of that dark tunnel!

We all know how difficult sustained change can be when tackling negative ingrained habits. We are going to need new positive habits. In order to change negative subconscious beliefs we need all the powerful mental habits we can get! Let's pump this up another level, step with me into the visualisation gym.

Visualisation

Visualisation is a mental tool that we can develop into a habit that can aid wish manifestation. We can use visualisation to strongly impress new images and therefore new beliefs onto our subconscious mind. Essentially visualisation is the formation of a mental image of goal accomplishment to a high degree of detail. Imagination is the ability or the means by which we are able to daydream and visualisation is the fine art of imagining.

Images are the individual words that we use to speak to our subconscious mind and so visualisation is the comprehensive language. Just like you would use your conscious thought to set your conscious mind a goal of acing an exam, you can use your visualisation to set your subconscious mind a deeper goal for it to work towards and bring about in your life.

Visualisation is a very strong manifestation tool used for many different purposes by many different people. Visualisation is often used in extremely high pressure situations by athletes, astronauts and grand prix winners. In motor-racing famous grand prix winners, such as Lewis Hamilton, have said when they fall behind on the race track what they do is switch gears, mentally that is. A part of their motor sports training is mental training in which their visualisation muscle is built up, so it can powerfully kick in during a high pressure situation. In a calm almost meditative state these drivers can mentally shift their energy from fear and panic to faithfully visualising themselves turning things around and winning the race. Hey presto would you believe it, they then ended up catching up and going on to win the race just like they visualised!

Like these high speed racers you too can use this mental tool to manifest your dreams and develop it into a habit. But you must ask yourself how strong are my visualisation skills? Can I build up my faith in this process enough so that I can calmly trust my wish is granted just like I visualise? Can I operate from that place of power? Does your visualisation produce for you feelings of elation because you just know you have already received your wish? Or do you panic and begin to doubt what you visualise, especially if you are under pressure?

Your confidence in your visualisation skills can be built up the same way you would build up body muscle, with exercise! Begin with small things like visualising getting good parking spots at a car park you often frequent. As you start to manifest more good parking spots than normal, gratefully take note of these results and then start to visualise manifesting bigger things. That is how you build up your confidence in the visualisation process so that like those racers you too can be calm and not worry.

These visualisation exercises should feel joyous because in them you are getting what you want. You should be experiencing the feeling of having your wishes, what does that finally feel like to have your dream?! Faith without action is dead because true faith will lead you to action. If you are constantly focused on worry, fear and doubt when you visualise then you are not acting in faith.

Why You Can't Think Straight

Speaking about worry, fear and doubt let's examine how these emotions can affect the wish manifestation process, and in fact our life. When we are going through challenges in life these can appear much worse to us because we then add on constant worry, doubt and fear. Worry, doubt and fear are negative emotions. Strongly feeling these negative emotions for a prolonged period of time produces ongoing stress on the body, the results of this being we cannot think straight, literally!

The definition of stress is a state of emotional or mental strain that results from being in demanding circumstances. Stress is the feeling of being under too much emotional or mental pressure. Stress means literally tension and also wear and tear. What do you think will happen in your body if you always have stress?

There are real physiological reasons why we cannot think clearly whilst experiencing ongoing stress. Everything in our being is connected. When we step away from focusing on fear the effect in our body will be that the amygdala (the emotions centre) in our brain is no longer working overtime. This is really good because it means the stress hormone, cortisol, will cease from causing ongoing damage to the neurons in our brain. Neurons are specialized cells in the brain and their main function is to transmit information, mentally connecting the dots so to speak. Now stress hormones aren't always harmful to the body but they do tend to cause damage when they are being over produced. Ongoing stress causes real physical damage to our neurons which produces the effect of us literally not being able to think straight. Because of neuron damage ongoing stress literally impairs our brain's ability to connect the dots, it degrades creative neural pathways along with other harmful effects in the body. So you can see why it makes sense to go in the opposite direction of focusing on fear.

The good news is when you make the decision to shift from a position of fear the opposite of all of this will happen. Many good things happen physiologically in your body when you choose to focus on positive emotions, your neurons are happy and creativity flows.

Now we know some of the biology behind how focusing on fear and negative emotions ultimately degrades the body. The question now is when you find yourself in a challenging situation, as is inevitable in life, do you want to approach it from a position of fear? That is do you want to operate from a position of weakness or of strength?

To approach challenges from a position of strength start by putting things into context. Start putting your focus on appreciating the safeties and securities (e.g. a family, a bed, good health) that you have already had for years. This will make you feel less scared and will start you going in the opposite direction to fear. By making this mental shift you will also ground yourself so you start to really feel the Universal support you have always had.

During this wish manifestation process you must be objective and know you have power over your mind. As a human being you must understand you are not your mind, your will is superior to your mind. Your mind serves you just as your body does. Both of these servants must be directed according to the language that they speak. You can use your will to calm your mind's fears when you understand how your mind works.

Objectivity

Objectivity involves having an open mind and considering all valid facts, rather than personal feelings, before deciding upon a course of action. Thinking objectively is a strong position be in throughout life because it facilitates your growth and emotional maturity. Practicing objectivity gives you empathy, the ability to understand others feelings. When you are objective in matters it allows you to be more fair because you take the time to understand yourself and others.

Being objective removes you from a purely emotional stance, being subjective is the opposite of being objective. When someone thinks subjectively they are constantly a slave to their own emotions and they have a small minded perspective because they can only see things from their point of view.

When you use imagination and visualisation to see yourself out of a challenging situation and stepping into your dream life, you become instantly objective as you mentally set yourself apart from that challenging situation. This means, you are no longer so caught up in the story of what is happening to you in your current life experience. This is great because you start to see that current circumstances are only your current reality and these do not define you.

Even if you don't have faith at the start of this wish manifestation process, if you can just be objective and have an open mind then faith can grow. Objectivity is just being open to a different perspective, through which a small spark of believing can start to creep in. Again we see everything is interrelated because as you hold on to this small spark it will grow and fear will shrink. You will start to be able to look at things less emotionally and more logically. On an energetic level you make a shift and so the frequencies you emit will change. You start going in the opposite direction, you shift gears! Everything is connected so making a change in one area affects everything else. But to let all of this magnificence in you must first be open!

The power that lies in taking the objective approach can assist you in so many ways on this wish manifestation journey. Life can be challenging, but you must allow yourself to dream new dreams regardless of past disappointments.

Keep your eyes focused forward because your past and current circumstances do not define who you are. Perhaps there have been big disappointments along the way in your life so now you don't dream anymore. But objectively looking back now can you honestly say, knowing what you know now, that you are still really surprised that your dreams didn't work out at the time? C'mon, give yourself a break! If you would have known better at the time then of course you would have done better. And now you do know better so proceed on that basis! Be objective and fair to yourself, beating yourself up is not going to empower in anyway it will only subtract from your power.

In life and on this wish manifestation journey it is very useful to be objective because not every desire is going to be realised. Life works in mysterious ways and for whatever reason not all dreams are meant to come true. Some dreams can actually only to come to life from the ashes of dreams that didn't quite work out. Dreams that didn't come to fruition can lead you to walk the path of self-mastery, on this path it is only when you turn around and look back will the series of near misses then make sense. Your series of near misses have propelled you on an ongoing quest in which you are constantly sharpening your skills by being spending more time on the leading edge of the life's experience. You become like "The Greatest" boxer Mohammed Ali getting back up in the ring time after time, you hone your skills! Now I'm not trying to sell you a line here, a sort of get out clause as to why not all dreams come true, I'm forging meaning from pain and disappointments. Forging meaning from heartache does not make what has hurt us right, it makes what has hurt us precious because we can learn something from it.

So don't lose hope, take an objective perspective, if you got everything you wanted straight away in life then you might be bored! You wouldn't really have a gripping story to tell and isn't overcoming challenges a big part of what life is about, isn't that what makes it an exciting adventure. The key here, as the famous song goes, is to "Don't Stop Believing!" If a dream or two doesn't work out, despite you really trying, learn to humbly surrender all but don't give up on the process as a whole. Accept that for whatever reason this dream in particular wasn't meant for you and then go ahead and dream another dream.

When you feel like giving up entirely and you are about to say to yourself "Dreams don't come true!" Just be objective and remember Thomas Edison, the inventor of the light bulb, tried and tried and did not get it right 10,000 times!

Be objective and remember the law of attraction might actually be **so close** in delivering your dream to you but if you say "This silly dream stuff doesn't work!" Then as you know by now, that is exactly what you will get.

Trust! Be objective! Have faith and believe in the creative process till the day breaks and the shadows flee away.

Shine Bright Like the Star You Are

There is an order to this Universe and a set time for things, as we saw earlier on actions lead to reactions and with everything being connected there is a lot going on cosmically. Because you experienced past disappointments, for whatever reason, that does not mean you are doomed and you should stop trying and dreaming. Setbacks do not mean there is something inherently wrong with you. It does not mean everybody else deserves their dreams but somehow you don't. It does not mean you are unworthy or unloved.

As you are now, you are a magnificent wonder the world has never seen before and will never ever see again! So seize the day! Give your genie the power that it needs to get strong so it can make you shine bright like the star that you are!

Play Dream and Imagine

Are you starting to get a sense of what you could have in this lifetime? If you truly understood what powers that you already have inside you and follow the natural laws, you could have heaven here on earth!

So don't sell yourself short in this life Play, Dream and Imagine! Be Bold! Ask Big! Live Big! Have the guts to believe you can have what you want! Why not? That is what you are here for! To experience life's joys to grow even bigger! Do not limit yourself! The more freedom you give yourself to imagine and dream new dreams, the more dream realities you could potentially get to experience!

A Special Note

Dear reader, we've covered a lot of ground in this section because you have a lot of innate power and many priceless gifts at your disposal. They just must be understood in order to be used for wish manifestation.

To conclude, essentially there are two paths in life. One path is to continue to set our sights upon the darkness and the other path is to make a shift towards the light. To make a shift towards the light you have to be able to focus on the light. With your will you can change paths at any time, naturally each path will produce different life results.

Changing paths can be difficult and will require consistent effort. Often a new positive image of yourself is the fuel required to start to change direction. 3 Wishes hopes to help give you that new positive image of yourself in the pages of this book. Will you choose to shift gears with us?

WORD TO THE WISE

Things are not always as they seem, here are some observations to note.

What are You Feeding Yourself?

With what we have covered so far in this book ask yourself the following questions. What have I been visually feeding myself and therefore exposing my heart to? Am I happy where I am in life and could this have anything to do with my subconscious beliefs? Do I have a vision for myself? Is there a disconnect between my internal authentic self and my external self out in the world?

Do not let these intimate revelations worry you. Your new awareness will bring you truth. The truth will allow you the opportunity to correct all errors in your mind. Also as you become enlightened from your new awareness, you instantly become more in control.

You now comprehend the power that lies in using images to give you a personal vision. You can also use the power in images to project what you want for yourself and align your natural energy flow. Using that same power of images that may have unconsciously kept you in fear and always stressed out, you can now turn that all around and use that power to make you a champion! Using the tools mentioned in this book you can use images to take active steps towards your dreams and you can change your life! Feed yourself those tools and images!

Just like we eat everyday to sustain our physical bodies so too must we feed our genie, or spiritual being, on the inside daily to really thrive. We can build up our genie in many ways through positive messages, positive images, positive self-talk and watching stories that inspire us.

We must also feed our dreams to make them strong, so write them down, map them out, colour them in, talk about them out loud even if it's just to yourself! Let them out!! Your natural energy flow must all be in alignment with your passions. Remember as above so below, do not pinch your energy off.

Regardless of your current circumstances let a part of your focus be on playing make believe like you once did as a child, trusting in your dream and knowing that YES the spectacular Universe will fill in the blanks. It is not your job to worry about if your wish is going to come true or not; we have already seen how stress and fear is counter productive. Refuse to become disempowered by feeding yourself fear.

Say finances is the issue regardless of your bank account status do not feed fear. It is not your job to always speak of lack or to focus on the opposite of what it is you actually want. The law of attraction is absolute if you always speak words like "I'm terrible with money." "I'm broke." "Lord, let me just make it to the end of the week!" Then guess what? That is exactly what you will get and attract, you will just make it to the end of the week and no more! Don't you want more than that?

What words are you feeding yourself? What language do you use when you talk about yourself to others? People don't realise when they complain all the time and speak negatively they are unknowingly speaking those things into existence. Be aware your spoken words in addition to your thoughts are very powerful!

It's Just around the Corner

Where most people get stuck is because they can never really **see** themselves in their dream state living their dream life, well they just don't believe their dream could be possible for them. Again you come from the Source of All Creation! So YES wish fulfilment is very possible for you, nothing is impossible for you. You just have to confidently know what you are doing.

You want to become so saturated in believing in your dreams that you are not even able to relax unless you are working towards them in some fashion. That is when you know your genie has become strong on the inside and is flexing their muscles. Because at this point you just know that it is going to happen, do not be surprised when you start to see signs of your wish coming into your reality. This is because energies are staring to come into alignment, the Universe is responding to your command!

These could be first small signs which means the big stuff is just around the corner. This is confirmation that you are indeed on the right track so keep going. A small sign could be a word someone says that is along the same lines of business idea you received inspired thought on. You can use these small signs as fuel to keep going or even use them to tweak your idea, signs show you the Universe has got your back and is listening.

Along this wish manifestation journey you may lose faith at times falling back into old negative habits as dreams can take a while to manifest. Do not be hard on yourself if you go off track, remember to be kind to yourself during this process. It is okay, life happens. We all falter but to save the energy you have already invested in the process and to keep up your energy momentum you must get back on track as soon as possible. You see you must discipline yourself to get promptly re-dedicated and re-focused even if you had a setback and you don't really feel like putting the effort in.

And it is possible to get back on track because now you are objective enough to know that you are not your thoughts or your feelings. Thoughts and emotions come and go, you remain. You are in control of your emotions because you know you can make the choice to switch your thoughts, thus changing your emotions and feelings. This discipline will take some practice but you will get there, it's like working out at the emotions gym. Just like at a normal gym a little down time every now and then is fine, but if you take weeks or months off you will lose that definition in your abs that you worked so hard to create.

Even if your wish manifestation process does take a long time you will get the side benefits that come along with building up a new positive image of yourself. By focusing on the light you are also meditating on values like positivity, beauty, art, kindness, integrity and abundance. You can see that focusing on the dark can only bring you more pain, so you shift your focus away from that and begin to empower yourself. Regardless of your progress you will see this process is really worth it because it is also an energy healing process that will manifest personal development results in your life. So feel good! You are no longer stuck in that confused and hopeless place. Now you have hope, now you are striving to be better, now you have a plan and now you think and know that you too matter.

Others may not understand what you are doing, that's okay you are not here to spend your energy convincing them of this and that. Eventually they will see there is something different about you and the manifested results in your life. Sure, encouragement and feedback from others is nice and it does build confidence. But you must always know, regardless of whether you get this external assurance from others or not, that you have your own magical power inside you and by staying on the light path you are getting stronger!

Results in Different Packaging

Along life's journey things don't always pan out the way we expect them to. Very often we see people get their desires but getting to them by taking different routes. Or perhaps their dreams show up in different packaging, meaning their dreams are answered but not quite as you would expect.

Along these same lines we have to be very clear in what we ask for, because you could ask the Universe for an experience expecting one thing but get another. Say you ask for love, you may expect it to come to you in the form of a loving partner. But the Universe may send you love in the packaging of the experience of a rotten relationship, through which you really need to learn how to love yourself in order to survive it. This is why getting crystal clear is really useful!

The Landfill Harmonics story is good example of results in different packaging. In Cateura, Paraguay there is a small slum town where people literally live on a landfill site. Yet Favio Chavez had a dream of making beautiful classical music and conducting symphonies by forming a youth orchestra in this place. Now because of the very real circumstances of poverty these folks live in they could have all thought, "What's the point in this crazy dream? The big city and everything around us tells us that we are poor. My father was poor, my grandfather was poor and so I will always be poor! We don't have money so how could we ever make this beautiful music?!" They would have never made music with those negative thoughts because those self-defeating thoughts would have paralysed mentally them before they even just tried!

Well regardless of their physical surroundings they did not see themselves as victims! Instead, they chose to see themselves in the light of an abundant self-image and they saw themselves creating that beautiful classical music. They directed their thoughts, attention and emotions towards what they wanted and not towards what they didn't want. They decided they knew their wish was actually possible for them, regardless of their circumstances and poor surroundings. Their thoughts were, we **can** make this music! This belief and strong faith in their vision influenced their frame of mind making them become resourceful with ideas. That confident mental perspective led them to start to look about for resources around them that they could use to help them accomplish their dream. Chavez had the genius idea of using the garbage around them in the landfill to actually make the musical instruments! Instruments like cellos and violins were all made from "trash" others had thrown away in the landfill. Literally one man's trash is another man's treasure here because this "trash" even elevated this group of spirited people to fame and fortune!

Today the Recycled Orchestra is a world famous classical musical group that put their small town Cateura on the world map! They now travel the world touring and performing for captivated audiences, award-winning movies have even been made about their story. You see how their dream got elevated even higher than their initial vision of playing music just for their town folk. This group of champions have become a source of inspiration to many internationally.

That extra blessing of fame would not have happened to them to the same degree if they had just raised some money and bought some new instruments and made music. Sometimes what could be considered by some as a disadvantage, is actually what is going to propel you and your dreams even further than you can imagine. These people were starting from a massive disadvantage but they still overcame the odds. Just imagine what you can do!

In the wish manifestation process it is important to be open to the mysteries of life, practicing gratitude along the way whilst objectively keeping an eye on the bigger picture.

YOUR MAGNIFICENT POWER STATION

This section is dedicated to how you can put yourself in the best possible position to make your wishes come true. How does one go about doing this? By getting your energy right!

If things haven't been going well for long time and you really can't see why it can start to feel very frustrating. It is helpful to understand the nature of your own energy and how you can consciously manipulate it in order to change your life experience. This all comes down to how we manage our energy.

We are Energy

This book began by stating everything in the Universe is energy. By nature humans are energy generators which is why the power station analogy is used here. We are power stations that can use many different types of fuel to produce many different types of energy. A power station needs it's fuel maintained at certain levels in order to avoid power outages, so too do we need our generators maintained at certain levels to avoid shut down. Imagine you are the owner of a magnificent power station, which indeed you already are, wouldn't you want to do all that you can to run your station at optimal capacity?

When you are ready to see real change in your life, radical action is required in order to transform old energy patterns that did not serve you. Think about it in terms of energy momentum, to slow down a high speed train going in a certain direction you will need an equal opposite force. Your old energy patterns, which stemmed from your habituated thoughts, feelings and subconscious beliefs, are what have brought you to where you are now. The old patterns of being may have ended up bringing you what you don't want, so the old ways must be surrendered and cast off like a snake shedding it's skin.

Why so radical? Well the definition of madness is doing the same thing over and over again, yet each time expecting a different result. The same way a woman cannot be a little bit pregnant to give birth to a new life, you too cannot be a little bit committed to change in order to bring about a new life for yourself.

You may feel miserable in your everyday life and not know why. Just take note that this is your emotional guidance system feeding back to you that somewhere along the line your energy patterns are off and need adjustment, so it's time to send in the engineer! To tune up our energy patterns they need to be brought back into alignment with truth and light. And we can get to the truth by asking questions and pursuing knowledge.

What is the first question that is asked when sitting down to play a game? What are the rules?! Would you want to play a game without knowing the rules? How far could anyone get without knowing the rules of a game? Not very far, they wouldn't even stand a chance of winning! This is why knowledge is power. Energy has it's own natural laws, like karma etc., and you must know these rules in order to successfully play this game of life that is all about energy.

When Planting Roses

Are you struggling with the concept that your current circumstances are really a result of your past thoughts and subconscious beliefs? This is a natural response to the truth don't worry. This resistance is your frightened ego's defence mechanism. Your ego wants to fight back because your will is about to shatter it's familiar reality with some truth. Do not be fooled by your ego it knows many, many, many tricks. Ultimately we are spiritual beings having a human experience, so in order to evolve we want to be guided by spirit and not driven by ego.

Perhaps you are confused because the results in your life are not what you consciously want? Often because we unconsciously operate from a position of fear what we actually manifest is our fears, or the opposite of what we actually want! This is natural law justice, it shows in every way similar energy does match up!

As you take time to pause and deeply reflect on your past, are things starting to make sense? Is it starting to really dawn upon you that your current experience could be a residual effect of the energy patterns you generated in the past? Along with this realisation should also come the insight that therefore, by this reasoning, you are in effect not doomed to be perpetually defined by your current circumstances, this is just an accumulation of who you used to be.

When you fully comprehend these realisations you have an aha moment, a moment of clarity in which a heavy weight will lift up off you. You enter a higher state of knowing, a higher state of being, you elevate to a new energy field. Once you have started on this path it is possible to willingly continue to shift your energy patterns. It is possible to elevate yourself to an even higher frequency and reach a higher ground. By always focusing on the light you can eventually get from where you are to where you want to be.

When planting roses you need to select the right type of soil for those roses to be able to grow and beautifully bloom. Likewise your own energy needs to be just right for your dreams to grow and manifest. You can only make this selection if you are aware of what type of energy you are working with. If you have had power outages in the past, some real soul searching will be required to find out what was the root cause that made your power station malfunction.

Ask yourself the following soul searching questions, really think about your answers and then write them down. Do you really want your dream life? Do you believe you deserve it? Do you believe you deserve happiness? If you discover really deep down that you don't believe you deserve your dreams then why could that be? Are you really ready to let go of negative habits so that you can move towards your dreams? Are you ready to let go of heavy emotions like blame, unforgiveness, resentment and fear? Are you really sick and tired of being sick and tired? Are you ready to stop making excuses and do all that you can to get your dream life? Are you ready to stop looking back all the time and instead set your sights towards the future? Are you ready to fight for your own dreams or will you shrug off your responsibilities and put someone else in charge of your own happiness?

Now if you did it right then that was a big emotional exercise you just did so take a breath, maybe lie down for a bit while you process.

Those were introspective questions that will help you understand yourself and why you do the things you do or exhibit certain energy patterns and behaviours. Becoming self-aware is the key to unlock emotional growth. Growth is ultimately why we are all here, this is our real spiritual work. Evolution does not come without growing pains, change is not easy so I take my hat off to you and commend your bravery!

Well Done You!

My dear reader, do you know how far you have already come just by having an open mind whilst you read this book, mulling over it's content? Let's take a moment to reflect on just how far you have come.

You have already taken action towards change by investing in yourself and getting this book too! You have already woken up from the mass scrolling hypnotism of modern-day life because you are now purposefully listening to and connecting with your wise heart! You have already given thought to what dreams you want to accomplish in this lifetime! Now you know how energy works, you find you are not becoming so easily distracted by what everyone else is doing on social media! Because you are now aware of the power that lies in just your focus alone, your attention is not being so easily stolen by fake news or celebrity gossip headlines! Your focus, and therefore your energy, is not being squandered and invested in some soap opera drama of mindless leaders!

Well done you!!! Give yourself a round of applause! Really, in order to stay motivated on this journey you will need to be able to encourage yourself even with the small victories. Take no shame in being your own 24/7 cheerleader!! Being able to encourage yourself and practice positive self-talk will boost your chances of success and charge up your power station.

Guard Your Heart

Above all things you must guard your precious heart, because everything you do flows from it. Be selective of what you expose yourself to visually and watch who you let influence your concept of self. People trampling all over someone's heart is how their self-esteem gets tampered with in the first place. Your heart is going to be open during this time of shifting energy patterns and healing so do remember to protect it.

Guarding your heart also means you must monitor how you use your energy to ensure you have enough reserves to put towards your wish manifestation. All these new ways of being; the asking, visualising, believing and then taking action, all of these activities will require your focused energy and time.

Being Vulnerable

Opening your heart up so that your dreams can come true involves an element of allowing yourself to be vulnerable. Vulnerability does require your concentrated energy because it involves the dismantling of habituated self-defence mechanisms such as cynicism. Being vulnerable means accepting that you may not actually know everything after all and perhaps you do need some wisdom, as we all do.

Being vulnerable involves pausing, reflecting and being honest about the signs of pain showing up in your life. Pain can be so deep in your being that you are not even consciously aware that you are in fact hurting somewhere. This is because along the way, a long time ago, you learned to bury that pain. But my dear the energy of that pain is still very much present in your life today. Until your pain is addressed and healed it will keep on cropping up and manifesting itself in different ways your life. Remember everything is energy, this includes pain, and energy can never be destroyed it can however be transformed through healing.

To fix an energy leak in a power station you must first find out where the leak is. In order to heal a wound you must first address where you are hurting. When you acknowledge what caused the wound you can then start the work of healing. You don't have to do this healing alone there are so many things that can help your emotional body heal. After thoroughly dealing with the main issue you can get on the path of recuperation by watching funny movies that make you laugh, reading healing books, seeking out wisdom and understanding, watching inspiring videos, getting out in the masterpiece of nature, exercise, doing yoga and using the healing energy of crystals. There are so many healing energies around us! Surround yourself with these healing things, spend your time with people that make you feel uplifted and not diminished. To be able to move forward and get unstuck energetically, you must first open yourself up to let all of these healing energies into your heart. They can't get in and help unless you make the conscious decision to let your walls of defence down.

Shaking off disappointments does call for a lot of energy, especially if you have experienced years of confusing disappointments. Disillusionment can start to set in and I want to personally say I know how hard it is to open up your heart again, trusting and believing again after many setbacks. This is being vulnerable. I want to tell you I really understand that feeling of being lost in despair and hopelessness. If your heart is broken now that is okay, you are not expected to just snap out of it. If that is the case then what you can do is just start off by taking small baby steps towards the light everyday. Approach things the easy way. If change scares you keep to your normal routine, but do try to do just one small thing everyday that shifts you towards your dream and towards the light. This one small thing could be even just looking at your wish image for thirty seconds daily, do this before you start to build up to other things.

But you must open up there is no other way to see change in your life if you do not open up and make a shift. You may think "Well should I try again now?" The difference between the past and now is, now you are actually aware of what you are doing and you know how to work with energy. Infinite Intelligence will meet you where you are at and walk with you every step of the way, carrying you with grace when you are tired.

If you are ready to take radical action right now to make a big energy shift great. If your emotional body has been through a lot and you cannot be so vulnerable right now, then that is alright too. Be kind and listen to your self. Perhaps your work right now is just to get back on even emotional ground first, so do that before you start to build up. Even if your steps are tiny, the important thing here is that you start the shift because in the starting you take your energy patterns in a different direction. Remember it is never too late to start.

Keeping Things On Point

You must run your power station efficiently and wisely cutting back on energy wasted on grudges, distractions and fear. Ultimately in order to heal you must rebalance and realign your emotional, spiritual and physical bodies. To get your energy in alignment with your dreams you must use your will to take back the power that has always been yours. You must come up with a real emotional plan on how you are going to get to that light at the end of the tunnel. You must start to do better for yourself now so you can start to have better in your life. You must believe you can have more for yourself in order to be able to get it! You must expect good things in order to get good things. You must push yourself to be responsible for the energy you bring to the table because this has very real effects upon your life. Energy does not transform through making excuses or by blaming others. You have to take control of your energy and you have the power to do this because you it is your birthright as a creator!

Why should you do all this you may ask? Well, don't you want to live a magical life that one day you can look back in wonder at and say WOW…did I do all that?

Prioritising keeping your power station on point will better enable you to manifest your wishes. As the saying goes if you stay ready then you don't have to get ready. When you receive inspired thought on how to manifest your dreams, in order to be able to act swiftly upon it you must empower yourself to be ever ready to step wholeheartedly into new opportunities. Your energy must be right. This will require an element of being able to shake off disappointments quickly and being vulnerable. The reality is the quicker you can get back on track and keep up your momentum, the faster you will get to your dreams. The natural laws are absolute.

Go on a Love Diet

We have seen how soul-searching and being vulnerable will require concentrated energy when managing your power station. So what can you do to turbo charge your power station? Love, love, love!

Love is a super elixir!! Think about it, love does make you feel stronger because it gives you more energy. Suddenly you have the power to do things you wouldn't normally do, all at once you have the stamina to drive all night to go see your love, yes indeed we can do anything for love.

So we know love has super energy inside it, how can we then use this and put more love in our lives in a way that is not dependent upon other people? In a sense to build yourself up! What you can do is to develop a regular self-loving practice in which you are engaging in things that fill you up with that feeling of love and feeling good.

Some powerful self-loving practices are falling asleep listening to positive affirmations, having daily positive mantras, taking care of yourself and doing mindfulness breathing practices when you feel anxious. Be kind, understanding and compassionate when you deal with yourself, these are all manifestations of love.

You deserve all the good things in life! Remind yourself that you are trying and that you do in fact deserve your own kindness, understanding and compassion. Nobody is capable of instantly transforming their entire energy overnight so do not judge yourself if change takes a while. If you have a setback into your old unconscious habits just take note of the setback and be kind to yourself. That way you will know what to avoid or be on the look out for next time.

Anytime you feel down think about what caused you to come down off your good vibes? You may sense the setback was triggered by someone from your past bringing you down, for example an ex-partner that is still really caught up in your old frequency. Pay attention to how your own energy feels after any interactions with them, old energies and new energies don't tend to mix well so you may feel really drained after.

Because you are now on a love diet and building yourself up you want to avoid any energy drain as much as possible. So limit your time spent with that person or change the way you interact with them, or cut them out completely just like you would do on a regular diet. Do not try to reason too much with people on lower frequencies, you desperately trying to help them see sense can drag you down into a bottomless pit! Just leave these energy vampires to it! Bless them, they just don't get it and they often don't even want to try get it. Everyone is not on the same evolution schedule and that is okay.

Nobody has the right to steal your joy so do not give it to them! You are here to thrive really feeling good and from that feeling good comes the opportunity to live your dreams. Every time someone brings you down what is happening is that they are in fact stealing your energy and taking you away from your dreams! Do not allow that! That's right you have permission to rise above and lovingly put yourself first!

Concentrate your own focus on you and you thinking and doing positive things, this will nurture you and build you up. Cast your sights on principles of the light like honour, self-respect, purpose, integrity and dignity, meditate on all of these good things. Building up your self-esteem is always a good thing whether you are chasing your dreams or not.

Love is the essential fuel we all need in life and we will need even more supplies of it when we are striving towards a precious dream. So receive all of the good stuff that makes you feel good with both hands! Take all the compliments, appreciation, I love Yous, kisses, hugs, smiles, gifts, cards, flowers and self-loving you can get!

Set Yourself Up for Success

Set yourself up for success during this precious period of building up your energy, healing and working towards your dreams. Really think about it, when you go into surgery to get a body part fixed, you don't take your phone in or bring your friends into theatre with you. Whilst you are recuperating in hospital the nurses will limit your visitors so you can save your energy and put your whole focus towards healing. This is the same wise way you must be when doing this energy work. On this wish manifestation journey you will be addressing deep-rooted issues such as why your self-image and energy patterns are the way they are. So a lot of your energy will be spent on self-reflection and focusing your attention inwards.

Everything emits it's own particular energy signature. Stop and think about where you go to and what type of places you frequent? If you feel drained after you go somewhere sometimes you need to stop and think, what is it about this place I go to that when I leave there my energy feels depleted? I felt fine before. Energy is always being exchanged, so analyse how a place may affect you and make an effort to go to places of beauty that inspire and lift you up.

Be aware this is a vulnerable time for you as your heart is going to be opening up and healing from past hurts, so you really need to think about what you are doing on a day to day basis. Set yourself up for success by paying attention to the finer details in your daily life and how you spend your energy.

Recognise quickly what emotions are going to drain you and cut them off quickly. Be quick to forgive and let go of offences swiftly before they fester. Forgiveness is really for yourself because holding on to grudges, or even trying to really get to the bottom of why someone did you wrong, will derail your thoughts. As your thoughts get derailed well there goes your energy, you are no longer really focused on the good things that you want. When you carry around unforgiveness what you are transmitting to the Universe, on a subconscious belief level, is somebody owes me something! This negative energy can manifest itself in many ways in your life, even leading you into financial debt. Ask yourself is that grudge really worth it? Ask yourself what matters more to you in this life; living your dreams because you can put your whole energy towards them or splitting up your energy just so you can hold onto a grudge? A grudge that the perpetrator probably does not even think about! Beware unforgiveness can really become all consuming and ruin your chances of success.

If you focus on and define yourself solely by someone doing you wrong this gives you a victim not a victor mentality. A person with a victim mentality has energy patterns that are off. They will not be able to powerfully attract what they really want in life because they see themselves as weak and so they become a weak magnet. You manifestation and attraction skills will be very weak if you are projecting a victim self-image, so do what you can to let that go asap.

Brush that dirt off your shoulder! Depending on the aggrieved situation you can leave it up to the Universe to sort out those who have done you wrong. There are many natural energy laws like karma that can handle this for you. As the saying goes what goes around comes around. Say your piece then let it go, you can then turn your attention back onto yourself and focus on the awesome stuff you actually do want in life, seeing yourself as the champion that you are!

Always think in terms of the big energy picture. See your daily life in terms of energy at your power station and observe where you may be wasting any reserves. Ask yourself "Is this drama I'm currently involved in going to bless me and bring me closer to my dream? Is all this mess really worth my time and energy long term?" Balance your new streamlined focus with relaxation, peace and play and the life shift you will observe will truly be magnificent! Keep going in this direction and in time you will be look back and say "WOW! Was that really who I used to be? I am so far away from that place!"

Warning on Low Frequency Energies

As we discussed earlier different types of energy operate on different frequencies or vibrations. Positive thoughts and energies (e.g. love, compassion, forgiveness) operate on higher frequencies and negative thoughts and energies (e.g. hate, criticism, envy) operate on lower frequencies.

You constantly engaging in low vibration emotions like worry, fear or numbness will only breed more sadness at the end of the day. As you wean yourself off these energies you **will** start to feel stronger. So why not do yourself a kindness now and start to turn away from those low frequencies that make you feel bad? Start going in the opposite direction from them, move from the darkness towards the light. Keeping your eyes focused upon the light and meditating upon it will show you how to keep on moving in that direction because that light will get brighter with time. Remember whatever you focus upon will grow.

Perhaps you are mentally stuck and you really do not know how to change direction. This is often just because you are thinking the same type of thoughts over and over again in a loop. If you are stuck don't panic, imagine your mind is like a drinking glass full of dirty water. Now you don't need to worry about how you are going to get the dirty water out of that glass. All you need to do is to keep on pouring in clean water into that glass. As you continue pouring in clean water eventually the dirty water will spill out and what you will be left with is clean water. The same principle applies to our minds because our minds are like containers. It is up to us what type of thoughts, or water, we keep in our minds so just keep on pouring in the good stuff till the bad stuff goes.

Engage in positive activities that are going to boost your energy in your power station. Fun activities like art and colouring, activities that make you feel good, capable, creative and even cool! There is nothing cooler than practicing self-love, knowing your own self-worth and valuing yourself enough to know your dreams are important too.

You don't have to be afraid to really express yourself in these pages, this is your personal vision book made just for you! However maybe because of your environment you might feel like you need to protect your dreams at first. Just until they get strong so you may choose to keep this book to yourself just like a diary. By golly go for it, do whatever you need to do to grow your dreams nurturing them from seedlings everyday.

It is important you start to wake up from a world of low frequency energies and disengage yourself from the hypnotism of distractions, numbness and pain. Don't worry as you disengage from old habits you will not be left with nothing to do, you are swapping one type of energy for another.

As you start to run your power station differently you may lose people you thought were your friends, but as you evolve higher remember you are never alone in this. You actually make more room in your life for a better quality of wonderfulness and there are many Universal forces that will be with you along the way.

Maybe you don't believe in all of this "stuff". Okay, but aren't you just a little curious to at least to see what the results will be in your life if you really try things a different way? If the old way wasn't working anyway, then what do you have to lose? Go on, aren't you even just a little bit curious?

Practice Gratitude

Lastly super charge your magnificent power station by practicing gratitude. When manifesting gratitude is an essential practice because it invites in more abundance and prosperity into your life. Within reason take every opportunity that you can to practice gratitude, even if you don't really want that piece of gum accept it gracefully when offered.

This logic also applies to small things like even picking up pennies along your path walking down the street. Give thanks and feel that warm fuzzy sense of gratitude as you bow down to get those pennies. Do you know what these pennies mean and symbolise? These pennies mean the Universe thinks you are so awesome that it is sending you gifts of free money just as you walk down the street! Bear in mind that you are not even working at the time this is just for you strolling down a road. How awesome is that! What do you think is going to happen if you allow your unchecked ego to kick in causing you to ignore those pennies? Your ego may say to you, "I'm too big to pick up those pennies!" Do you ever think about what type of energy you are giving off as you turn your nose up at something? Think about it, what would you do if you tried sending someone small gifts but they always shunned them, wouldn't that make you want to stop? And would that make you want to send them bigger gifts?

Signs of Land

A long time ago when ships sailed for months on rough seas seeking out new lands, the explorers could never see the whole new island straight away. The entirety of the whole new land would never come into their focus straight away. What they would see first are signs of land like birds flying in the sky, and they would joyfully celebrate these signs for days before the whole new island fully came into focus.

That too is how we must be during this wish manifestation process, we must celebrate the little signs. As we have seen already there are a lot of factors at play in wish manifesting. It depends on where you are at in terms of your energy, your dedication, your faith and the right thing happening at the right time.

Just be patient bearing in mind that all of these factors could affect your results.

Your wish manifesting results may come quickly or like planting a tree and waiting for it to grow it may take a while. But along the way just be grateful for your journey towards the light. Celebrate! Because even though you may not be quite where you want to be yet, you are nowhere near that dark confused place you used to be stuck at.

Now you understand yourself more and you know what you are working with. Now you have a plan on how to run your magnificent power station. So make a toast to life! Because now you are setting your sights in life upon your heart desires! Love, and not fear, is your new driving force making to very possible for you to live much more exciting realities! With this knowledge and wisdom this is the first day of the rest of your life! You have only just begun to really live!

My 3 Wishes For You

My wish for you is that your wishes come true to your hearts content.

May 3 Wishes bring you new energy that breaks chains of fear, self-doubt, self-criticism and worry.

May you see yourself in a new loving light and live your life knowing your dreams are important too.

These are my 3 wishes for you and for us all.

HOW TO ACTIVATE YOUR WISH IMAGES

Finally let's discuss how to get the most out of your personalised wish images. As you can see 3 Wishes features personalised art wish images of you in your dream setting. Each wish image is repeated three times so you can get into your colouring and really feel your way closer to that sensation of your dream.

Practice, Practice then more Practice

These personalised wish images feature you centre stage in your dream or wish setting; this could be a dream job, dream body, dream hobby, dream home or maybe a dream trip. Repetition or practice, practice, practice is essential to get your wish image ingrained into your being allowing you to really feel it's reality.

The feeling you want to repeat is the feeling of you accepting that your wish image is real. When you look at your wish image it needs to feel like it has already happened and now you feel joyful and enthusiastic because you have that thing! This is because in the law of attraction, you have to feel the nature of a thing and believe you already have it in order to bring it into your life.

The repetition practice also involves seeing and feeling your wish image daily. With each wish image being replicated three times you could have one copy for your office, one copy for your fridge, or your folder etc. The point is to put your wish image up somewhere you can see it daily in your line of vision. That way you can make it a daily habit to remind yourself of what it is you want. You are also reminded to stay aligned with the energy of that thing until you have fully entered the receiving stage of having it. At the point when you believe it's yours you can let go and just trust the Universe will deliver one way or another.

"We are what we repeatedly do. Greatness then, is not an act, but a habit"

Aristotle / Durant

With this daily habit we want to reach the point where you feel your dreams so strongly and so intensely, that you can't help but be strongly compelled to feel that they are real and they are going to happen. When you reach this saturation point you don't need to keep on looking at your wish image daily because you now know your subconscious has accepted your instruction. At this point, when you have managed to convince yourself that your dream will happen, you can let go and wait for some inspired thought or action you can take towards your dream. Or perhaps it will just show up signed, sealed and delivered in your life. Either way just be patient and trust, you may not know the how at the start but the way will be shown to you. Doing it the right way that Universe made just for you will feel so good!

Trust in the Universe and all of this ancient wisdom passed down from generation to generation. Know that because you have acted on this knowledge it **will** show up for you somehow! You have followed the steps of clearly asking for something and faithfully aligning your own energy up to the matching energy of that thing so it will happen for you one way or another. Do not worry because according to knowledge which is hundreds of years old it must manifest!

It's in the Details

Let your imagination run wild in your wish image, soak it up with no fear! Imagine you actually are in the image, where will you go next in your dream car? What colour are the flowers in the next room of your dream home? Or on your dream holiday what colour are the beach towels that just a few feet away? Be so inside your wish image that in fact it's like you are in that picture looking out here! This high detail makes use of the visualisation tool mentioned earlier.

You want to use finer details in your image to work yourself up to a feeling point so strong that it feels like your wish image is your actual reality! Regardless of the current circumstance you are in now, when you look at your wish image you need to pretend you are already right there! You are IN that dream car, you are IN that dream house, imagine you are right there right NOW

To get immersed in the details you must get super engaged in your wish image filling it in with colour(give it your emotion) and feeling(give it your heart). So colour all of those details in! Colour away with shading, outlining or bedazzling! Good things happen physiologically in your body just through this hand-eye coordination alone. Our brains emit happy hormones like serotonin and oxytocin when we colour in and dream. So why not do more activities like this that make you feel happy and good? When you feel good your power station is operating at optimal capacity which increases your manifesting power so keep up those good vibes!

Remember the Universe is always listening out for your commands on what you want and your commands are being transmitted through your brainwaves. As discussed at the start of this book this works by your thoughts and feelings creating electromagnetic brainwaves which then send out a frequency to the Universe. The Universe listens to your transmitted frequency takes it as a command that this is what you want and sends back to you the matching life experience. The Universe is always listening out for the details you give it, the more detail you transmit the better the results!

So what does it feel like to own your dream home?! You may say out loud "I feel proud to be a home-owner!" "I feel responsible, I feel secure in my own duplex!" All of these are detailed emotions you need to work yourself up to feeling and really thinking about in order to immerse yourself in the details of your wish image.

This wish image immersion practice can also be done daily and then follow that up by feeling grateful for all that you already have. The immersion goal is that when you look at your wish image your belief in it needs to be built up to the level of even going ahead and giving thanks to Infinite Intelligence because you just know your wish has already been granted!

Example Using Repetition & Immersion

Let's look at repetition and immersion in practice, say your bank account is currently in the red. What to do is to focus daily on your wish image of yourself surrounded by symbols of riches. Study all the details of the wish image and say with conviction "Alright I may not have much in my account today but that is just temporary, so it doesn't mean anything long-term. I can clearly see it here, I know that I am rich!"

Keep on speaking your riches into existence! Give thanks for your riches! Claim prosperity by saying out loud "By day and by night I am being prospered in all my ways!" Continue this practice until you actually really feel rich! Don't stop there, there are so many ways to expand on your new rich self-image! Smell the money, imagine where you are going to drive to in your dream car. Add more colour and dimension make your personalised wish image BRIGHTER and BRIGHTER!!

Your job in the wish manifestation process is to enter that rich world mentally and emotionally trusting with all your heart that YES this is you! You want to believe in your new rich self-image so much that you are actually emitting feelings of financial abundance, to which the Universe will then respond to and manifest physical financial abundance in your life!

Again this is not to say that no planning or work is required on your part. When you truly think and feel rich on every level of your being, then you will have an abundance of ideas that can help bring you that financial abundance. Naturally you will want to take action on the inspired thought ideas to quickly bring that abundance into your life. Your whole energy, including your actions, will be in alignment with abundance once you accept abundance in your subconscious.

When you practice immersion and repetition your genie and dreams get invested in, and as they get fed they get stronger and stronger. You will find your everyday life becomes more colourful! Your belief that your dreams can come true for you starts to grow and hopelessness starts to shrink. Because you now know the truth and you are now open to new possibilities unexpected opportunities will come into your life! This all makes sense on an energetic level because you have in fact shifted your energy and you are now operating on a new energy field or frequency!

Be Still

Throughout this whole process it is important to learn how to be still. Learn how to block out all of the external and internal chatter so it becomes quiet, practice calmness and steadiness.

Your overall intent is to get from your current state to your dream state, or from an old self-image to a new self-image. This will involve intimately transforming false beliefs that have taken root in your subconscious mind so you must use your will to be still. Remember you manifest not what you want, you will manifest what you belief. The conditioning of false beliefs must be overcome because as we saw earlier whatever you deeply believe is what you will end up creating. You can overcome this delicate work more easily when you practice stillness.

When you are putting your ask out into the Universe calmly ask for the best possible solution and inspired thought. Your answer will probably come through and be interpreted by your mind. So it is better if you can still your mind to allow the answer to come through more easily.

When you really practice stillness then you could also gain access to the Universal Subconscious Mind and gain access to Universal Knowing. You can put yourself in a state to receive this knowledge by habituating being still. You have probably experienced some of this yourself when you are just relaxing or even half asleep and then poof! Solutions to problems or inspired thought will just pop into your head. Think about it, isn't it funny that this still state is when most inspired thought seems to come to people. When we are relaxed or in some state of stillness. Try this for yourself, just let go and let it come to you, think of yourself as a vessel tapping into a stream of creative consciousness.

To be still with your wish image it is a case of meditating on your wish image and then calmly, steadily and quietly just the Universe for guidance on how to bring this image into reality. There are many good forces in the Universe that want to assist us with our dreams if we would just ask, being trusting, open and humble.

When we are still and ask for the best possible solution to facilitate our dreams it is important that we do this from a place of stillness and power. Having trust and faith in our hearts gives us power, meaning we don't come at our endeavour from a place of fear, worry and lack. We saw earlier on how worry and fear are low energy frequencies that are bad for our power station.

Operating from a place of trust and faith, both of which are higher energies, will ensure you get the most abundant and prosperous version of your dream. So pause, be still and reflect, take a moment to be patient, to be mindful and listen out for that little loving voice inside that's trying hard to talk to you.

Meditate on Your Images

Coming from your heart space, meditate as you colour in yourself right there in your wish image. Get mentally lost in your image as you colour, breathe in deeply, breathe out deeply. Play some classical music as you colour in, block everything out so all there is you, your wish image and your dream. Drift away into dream land.

When you are done colouring really look at your wish image, then close your eyes holding that image in your mind's eye and meditate on that new vision of yourself daily for a few minutes. Close your eyes and really feel the reality of it. Give thanks to Infinite Intelligence that your wish has already been granted and give thanks for everything else in your life. Then come out of that, release it and go about your day.

X Marks The Spot

As you activate your wish images and listen out for your answer it is important to listen to intuition and trust in your sense of knowing. Is there any idea that pops into your head that seems kind of out the box? Anything unusual that makes you think, well where did that come from? That usually is the star inspiration you are looking for!

Don't talk yourself out it just because it has not been done before! An idea may come to you in the middle of the night, the ideas may not all come at once they may evolve. When the inspiration comes and hits the spot take action! Sit down and analyse the idea then make a plan and then take action following your plans through to completion.

The Wish Image Action Plan

See It by Keeping Your Wish Image in Front of You Always

Wholeheartedly Believe It has Happened, Giving Thanks & Letting Go

Listen out for the How and then Action It Through to Completion

Where To Put Your Images

These wish images will work best for you when you can see them all the time, that way they help keep you focused. It's all about your focus! Remember out of sight, out of mind.

How about printing your wish images on a daily item like your canvas bag? Or any other item to serve as a reminder during your day what your dreams are and what you are working towards. Perhaps even frame your personalised wish images in your home, making it a shared family goal and a regular topic of conversation speaking it further into existence. Sharing your dreams with like minded positive people amps up your manifestation power!

To really ingrain your wish image into your subconscious, strategically put it in a frame on your bedside cabinet! This way you are reminded to powerfully meditate on it before going to sleep at night! Our subconscious is most impressionable as we drift off to sleep and you mulling over your wish image as a mental movie as you fall asleep is a powerful practice. Remember you are trying to correct any negative subconscious beliefs and because these are deep rooted you need all the tricks you can get! Also this way your wish image in your bedside frame will be the first image you see to start your day when you awake. Set your intention for your day to work towards this new image of yourself in some way, you know that is some excellent motivation to make you want to get out of bed in the morning! You'll find you just can't wait to get out there and go get that dream and have your wish become your reality!

If you are trying to lose weight why not even make a t-shirt of your wish image showing you slimmed down to stay motivated at the gym or when working out at home. Go for it, there will only ever be one fabulous you!

Save your wish image on your phone and computer home screen. There are so many places you can place your image to make sure you are constantly exposed to it!

Social Media & 3 Wishes Community

The wish manifestation journey can be a deep and personal journey. It involves getting right to the heart of the matters. It can sometimes feel lonely and so do what you can to not lose motivation along the way. But as you have seen in this book you are never truly alone!

If you want to connect with like minded people do join our community on social media with #3WishesBook We'd love to hear from you ☺ Share your wish manifestation journey triumphs, results and challenges we are on Instagram @3wishespersonalisedbook

Follow and Like our Facebook page for posts, updates and videos. Our page is 3 Wishes Personalised Colouring Book Vision Board Tool We are also on YouTube just search for our 3 Wishes Book channel or watch our 3 Wishes book reviews videos from lovely YouTubers.

To help keep your energy momentum going and stay inspired sign up to our newsletter updates and check out our website by going to 3wishespersonalisedcolouringbook.com

Leave us a book review on Amazon or on our social media we'd like to hear what you think of this 3 Wishes!

Good Luck & Happy Dreamy Colouring!

Final Thoughts

Believe in you. Give yourself love first, as the love wells up inside you will then overflow and give real love to others. You absolutely must value yourself and believe that you deserve love! Flight attendants will tell you in the event of an emergency to put on your own oxygen mask first, because if you don't you will not be able to help anyone else. This is the same principle in life. You have to love yourself first before you can truly be in love with others. Some people feel more comfortable going above and beyond for others by pouring all of their energy into everyone else. But eventually, one way or another, the Universe will show you that you need to be balanced and invest in yourself. We cannot escape running our own power stations, the law of attraction teaches us we need to be for responsible for the energy that we bring to life.

Go to a mirror, that person looking back at you is the rescuer you have been waiting on! This whole time you have been walking around with your own personal hero. You have always had the power, you just had to learn it for yourself. You are a whole magnificent creator that can have any experience that you believe you can in life! You are not doomed, the only reason why you don't have what you want now is because you have not been playing this game of life by the rules. And now you have that wisdom.

What will manifest in life are the deep beliefs that you hold in your mind. Remember the iceberg analogy and the vastness of your subconscious mind that is underneath the water? To see real change you must delve into that deep water and intimately go where you have not consciously gone before. Your subconscious mind is your final frontier use your will to handle it. Your beliefs will shape everything in your life experience, really it is your subconscious beliefs that must be transformed to get what you actually want in life. You can transform your subconscious beliefs using Truth, Love, Wish images and the methods mentioned in this book. Keep healing yourself and pursuing the truth until you know and believe you deserve all of this and more! Do not be afraid my friend, as a creator you are here to dance your dance, you are already on the dance floor so just go for it!

"No one is free who has not obtained the empire of himself. No man is free who cannot command himself"

Pythagoras / Rowe

BIBLIOGRAPHY

Aristotle / Will Durant – Aristotle was an Ancient Greek philosopher and scientist. Durant summarized Aristotle's work from his book "Nicomachean Ethics" (349 BC) Book – Durant "The Story of Philosophy: The Lives and Opinions of the World's Greatest Philosophers" (1926)

Albert Einstein – Einstein was a German born theoretical physicist known widely for developing the theory of relativity and influencing the philosophy of science. Book - "Cosmic Religion and Other Opinions and Aphorisms" (1931)

Florence Scovel Shinn – Shinn was an American artist and book illustrator who then became a New Thought spiritual teacher and metaphysical writer. Book - "The Game of Life and How to Play It" (1925)

Pythagoras /Nicholas Rowe – Pythagoras was a Greek philosopher revered as a great scientist and mathematician. Rowe translated Pythagoras's quote from "Florilegium of Stobaeus Books 1 & 2" (5th Century AD)

Nikola Tesla – Tesla was a brilliant Serbian-American inventor, electrical engineer, mechanical engineer, physicist and futurist. Book - "The Problem of Increasing Human Energy" (1900)

Hermes Trismegistus / Balinas – In The Emerald Tablet Hermes referenced text that first appeared in Balinas's Arabic text "Book of the Secret of Creation and the Art of Nature" Book - "The Emerald Tablet" (An ancient text that first appeared in writings between the 6th and 8th century, original source unknown)

ABOUT THE AUTHOR

Like all of us, author A.O.K. has been on a journey of discovery and growth. Through the dust of ashes can come beauty and the strength to still rise.

A.O.K. studied Mindfulness at the Oxford University Mindfulness Center. Mindfulness themes have been woven into this book.

Made in the USA
Columbia, SC
16 October 2018